Lester Beall
Space, Time & Content

LESTER

Photo

War

modern

Pioneers in P

a

BEALL

Lester Beall
Space, Time & Content

BY R. ROGER REMINGTON

GRAPHIC DESIGN ARCHIVES
CHAPBOOK SERIES: ONE

RIT
CARY GRAPHIC ARTS PRESS
ROCHESTER, NEW YORK

2003

Lester Beall
Space, Time & Content
by R. Roger Remington

Copyright © 2003
Rochester Institute of Technology, Cary Graphic Arts Press
All rights reserved.

RIT Cary Graphic Arts Press
90 Lomb Memorial Drive
Rochester, New York 14623-5604
http://wally.rit.edu/cary/carypress.html

Front cover: Photograph by Philippe Halsman, c. 1946.
Copyright © Halsman Estate
R. Roger Remington's essay "Space, Time and Content,"
was adapted from his article published in *Eye* 24 (Spring 1997).

ISBN 0-9713459-8-8
Printed in Hong Kong

Library of Congress Cataloging-in-Publication Data

Remington, R. Roger.
    Lester Beall: space, time & content / by R. Roger Remington.
        p. cm. – (Graphic design archives chapbook series ; 1)
    ISBN 0-9713459-8-8 (pbk.)
    1. Beall, Lester, 1903- 2. Graphic arts–Private collections–New
York (State)–Rochester. 3. Rochester Institute of Technology–Art
collections. I. Title. II. Series.
    NC999.4.B43A4 2003
    741.6'092–dc21
            2003000632

Lester Beall

The art world is long on skills and short
on thought. It is wrong to believe that modern
design problems are solved by a series of
snap judgements. The answers must be found
now in hard work, hard thinking and
intensive objective study of everything from the
basic machinery which produces a product to
that product packaged and on the store shelf—
surrounded by literally thousands of other
products, each mutely clamoring for attention,
each trying to tell a preoccupied world
something, anything at all, about the contents
of the package and the people who made it.

'Good design' isn't good enough.
It has to be so soundly conceived,
so distinguished for the job it has to do,
that it has a quality of inevitability.

FOREWORD

Massimo Vignelli
April 16, 2001

HISTORY, THEORY AND CRITICISM: THESE WERE THE PASSWORDS launched at the first conference of Graphic Design History at Rochester Institute of Technology about 20 years ago. Until then very little or nothing at all had been done to document and study the development of Graphic Design in the USA. Times were ripe and Roger Remington of RIT spearheaded the efforts. Through his constant work, more conferences took place at RIT as well as across the country. You can be sure to find him in the auditorium or on the program of any event dedicated to history, theory and criticism. But his efforts and those of his colleagues at RIT do not stop with academic papers. The first archive of Graphic Design in the USA was the next step. One by one the archives of major designers, protagonists of the development of a new language of design were assembled, curated, protected, archived and documented.

The works of Ladislav Sutnar, Lester Beall, Will Burtin and others are now available to scholars at RIT, and this is a major event not yet followed by major institutions on a serious basis. My enthusiasm for this operation has been supporting the entire concept from day one and this publication represents the most recent effort by RIT staff dedicated to the documentation of Graphic Design.

Making a photogram, c. 1940
In his studio, Lester Beall mastered the photographic technique of making photograms and used these frequently in design solutions throughout his career.

Experimental photogram, 1940s
Photogram created in the 1940s from leaves and natural objects in Beall's studio.

Cover for ORS, 1950s
This design solution shows Beall's experimental photogram applied to the cover of a house organ for Davis and Geck. The publication was targeted for health professionals.

The format and size of this new series of books, dedicated to the designers in the RIT Graphic Design Special Collections, expresses the intention of reaching a wide audience of scholars and students, as well as design professionals. The intention is clearly that of increasing the awareness about the work of these masters and their impact on the development of the profession. It is the opportunity for assessing not only the value of their conceptual and formal talents but their moral and social responsibility as well. Far from being artists in a tower, all of them responded to their times with courage, a sense of commitment and professional dedication.

For these reasons, opening this new series of monographs with Lester Beall makes sense and I really hope that it will be received with enthusiasm by the audience. We are at a time of explosion in our profession. More and more young designers are reaching the market. For all of them, as for all of us, a detailed knowledge of the past is the only guarantee of a brilliant future. The new technologies have opened unimaginable possibilities for all of us, but the real task is not the education of the machine but that of its operator. The attempt by this series to fill the gap is a brave and timely effort in the spirit that fueled the Modern movement.

Keep going.

ABOUT THIS SERIES

Kari Horowicz
Art and Photography Librarian
RIT Wallace Library

THE GRAPHIC DESIGN ARCHIVES CHAPBOOK SERIES CELEBRATES the achievements of the key design pioneers found in the Graphic Design Archives of the Archives and Special Collections, Wallace Library, Rochester Institute of Technology.

The development of the Graphic Design Archives at the Wallace Library, Special Collections, began over ten years ago when Professor R. Roger Remington saw the need to secure and preserve graphic design collections. It is through Professor Remington's vision that these important collections have found a home at the Rochester Institute of Technology. Along with Roger Remington, Wallace Library's former Art and Photography Librarian, Barbara Polowy, saw to the proper care and access of the growing collections. The first collection bequeathed to Rochester Institute of Technology was the Lester Beall Collection in 1986. Since that time the Archives has grown to include sixteen collections. These collections focus on pioneers active between 1930 and 1960. Extensive collections of personal papers, business records and artwork by Lester Beall, Will Burtin, George Giusti, and Cipe Pineles form the cornerstones of the design holdings. Smaller collections include material documenting the works of Walter Allner, Hans Barschel, Alexey Brodovitch, Louis Danziger, Willam Golden, Leo Lionni, Alvin Lustig, Joyce Morrow, Paul Rand, Ladislav Sutnar, Ceil Smith Thayer, and Bradbury Thompson.

Lester Beall, c. 1963
At his Dumbarton Farm studio, Beall reviews a range of the various marks of identity he designed throughout his career.

The Archives support and enhance programs within RIT's College of Imaging Arts and Sciences, particularly the graphic design courses, but also drawing, illustration, packaging design, as well as editorial and advertising photography. The collections serve as catalysts for learning. Students and faculty use the collections to study the history of American graphic design and the history of editorial photography during a key period from the 1930s to the 1950s – a time of tremendous change and innovation.

In addition, the collections serve the international museum educational community. During the past five years, institutions such as the National Museum of American Art, Washington, DC, Maison Européenne de la Photographie, Paris, France, and the Museum Folkwangen, Essen, Germany, have borrowed materials from the Graphic Design Archives.

I would like to thank Massimo Vignelli for his initial suggestion for this series. Thanks to R. Roger Remington – the visionary behind the growing Graphic Design Archives here at RIT. I would also like to thank Professor Bruce Ian Meader for his expert publication design. A special thanks to David Pankow, Curator of the Cary Graphic Arts Collection and Editor of the Cary Graphic Arts Press, for his gentle enthusiasm and encouragement, and also to Amelia Hugill-Fontanel for her expertise as production editor.

It is only fitting that this first chapbook explore the work of Lester Beall since it is the founding collection of the holdings. In addition, Roger Remington is the authority on Lester Beall with several articles and publications devoted to Beall's life and work. With this inaugural publication we hope to encourage other graphic design historians to explore and enrich the vision of graphic design history and look forward to future chapbooks.

Lester Beall
Space, Time & Content

BY R. ROGER REMINGTON

NEW YORK CITY IN THE MID-1930S WAS A HEADY PLACE FOR creative people. Lester Beall, a member of a progressive group that included émigré European designers Alexey Brodovitch, Erik Nitsche, Joseph Binder, Josef Albers, Dr. M. F. Agha and George Salter, increasingly showed in his work the influence of the European avant-garde. More important than ever with the traditionalism of American graphics and advertising, he wrote, "My objection is to men thinking, during certain parts of the day, of streamlining trains, sub-stratosphere planes and super-charged autos, and then, during other parts of the day, mentally returning, misty-eyed and reverent, to the aesthetics of yesterday. For me, tradition handicaps while experimentation helps the creative artist."

Beall loathed the gimmicky nature of designs stimulated by the free-market capitalism of the time. He judged European artists and designers as successful in "shak[ing] off the shackles of the past." He was especially curious about the modernistic French machine aesthetic which he saw in the work from the Paris Exposition of Decorative Arts in 1925, which had promoted the design style that became known as Art Deco. Later, reflecting on this new form of Modernism, he wrote: "Good modern design in typography, as in the other arts, reflects the times in which we live, and because it does, it is firmly entrenched and is here to stay."

Photo Engraving, 1939
This cover, a Beall masterwork, exemplifies
the designer's power to synthesize
European influences and apply experimental
designs to jobs for pragmatic clients.
The use of angular type and antique
engravings superimposed by biomorphic
shapes, the mixing of typefaces and
type sizes, and the grouping of elements
recall the work of artists like Schwitters
and El Lissitzky.

Montage and photomontage became the major ways
with which Beall incorporated European influences into a
functional visual approach. "Photomontage allows subject
matter which is widely divergent in time, space and content
to be united in a single surface," wrote Anton Stankowski.
Looking back, Beall also found virtues in the synthesizing
properties of photomontage: "The desire to meet the challenge
of a new period in our economic and social history was
reflected by the ... search for forms that were strong, direct and
exciting." During this period he considered himself an
absorbent designer to whom the avant-garde had opened up
"a vast new field in which he could roam at random, plucking
blossoms haphazardly."

Beall had been interested in photography since his years in
Chicago when he most likely first saw a copy of the German
book *Es kommt der neue Fotograf*. He found this collection of
avant-garde still photography, published in 1929 when Beall was
26 years old, inspirational because it "took the camera off the
tripod and introduced to us [the American design community]
odd angles and bird's eye views and so forth." Photography
offered to Beall another representational imaging form to
complement his lifelong love of drawing. A tool was necessary
to preserve what he called "realism unadulterated." Impressed
by Moholy-Nagy's work with the photogram, Beall saw its
potential as offering "a unique ability to blend the abstract and
the fantastic with the real." In 1940, he wrote: "The development
of the camera in achieving organization and unity, combined
with the fact that the photograph per se represents the epitome
of 2D realistic reproduction, presents the graphic designer with
a powerful and moving instrument."

Photographic illustration for
What's New, c. 1939
To illustrate fever and dehydration for
this pharmaceutical piece for Abbott Labs,
Beall partially solarized the image.

Beall was fascinated by the flexibility of the medium, whose combinations, he said, were limited only by the "insuperable boundaries" of creative imagination. Photomontage became a natural way for him to combine his interests in photography, typography, art and printing with the revolutionary ideas about typographic form and page layout being propounded by El Lissitzky, Moholy-Nagy, Herbert Bayer, Ladislav Sutnar, Jan Tschichold and Man Ray. With this new direction, he became one of the major "construction image makers" among America's emerging designers.

The vocabulary of Beall's new visual language involved the use of graphic elements (color, form, texture, lines, gridded frames, geometric shapes); implied spatial structures (receding perspective lines, strong foreground/background relationships); typographic forms (bars, arrows, pointing fists, boldly mixed type styles, angled lines of type, masses of type set to conform to shapes); photographic processes (photomontage, studio photography negatives and prints, photograms, special lighting effects, silhouetted subjects, juxtaposed elements); and integrative effects and processes (collage, montage, simultaneity, spatial ambiguity, bold asymmetric balance with excessive use of negative space).

Of these variables, photomontage was the dominant unifying force because of the ease with which Beall could combine complex ideas. In Europe, photomontage had emerged boldly in the work of the Dadaists Raoul Hausmann, John Heartfield and George Grosz about the time of World War I and was, to Beall, "the first graphic reflection" of a new artistic consciousness. Other influences on the young medium were the cinematic effects of Sergei Eisenstein, new printing technologies that allowed the publication of photographic essays, the powerful visual forces of simultaneity in Pablo Picasso's Cubist works, Paul Klee's overlapping transparencies, Wassily Kandinsky's color and structure and the emergence of magazine photojournalism.

During this period, Beall experimented with many photomontage techniques in his studio. He glued together pieces of photographic prints, created multiple images in the darkroom, superimposed pre-existing images on new negatives, made double exposures in the camera and created photograms by placing objects directly on top of light-sensitive paper and exposing them. He frequently employed these procedures within the framework of basic integrating visual principles, such as multiple perspective and creative scaling.

Hitler's Nightmare, 1939
Beall designed this trade ad in 1939 for Crowell-Collier's magazine. It represented his excessive use of indexical arrow symbols in creating a powerful and timely message.

Will There Be War?, 1939
This second trade ad for *Collier's* achieved considerable visual strength through the ambiguity of sizes in the elements used.

Modern Pioneers in Peoria, 1937

Beall designed this title page and spread for a large-format promotional book, *Uncorking*, for Hiram Walker & Sons to promote their liquor products. The design is typical of Beall's style of the late 1930s and is one of his outstanding pieces of that period.

In 1936, Beall designed a cork-covered, spiral-bound promotional book for Hiram Walker, called *Uncorking*, which allowed him to play with photomontage. An outstanding example of the technique is shown in a spread called "Modern Pioneers in Peoria," which is so memorable that the entire book is sometimes known by that name. Beall's means of integrating illustration, carefully cropped photographs and type is dynamic and brings interest to the rather dull subject matter: a trip through a distillery. The maturity of his approach makes it distinct from the work of other pioneers of the time, including Alexey Brodovitch, Paul Rand and Bradbury Thompson. Although the printing quality was shoddy, the book design won a medal in the 1936 Art Directors Club of New York exhibition.

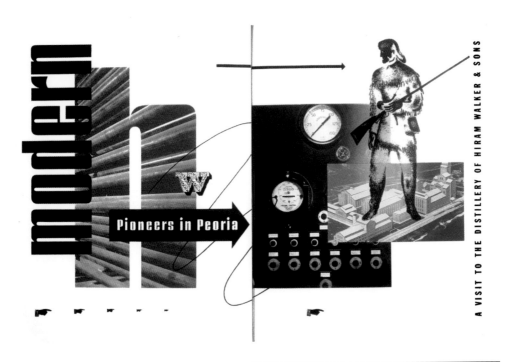

modern
Pioneers in Peoria

A VISIT TO THE DISTILLERY OF HIRAM WALKER & SONS

REA Series One poster, 1937
Wash Day

The purpose of these posters was to convince rural Americans of the advantages of having electricity in their homes.

Beall's growing reputation in New York owed much to an acclaimed poster series he had begun in 1937 for the United States Government's Rural Electrification Administration (REA), a part of the Department of Agriculture. Though electricity was first introduced to American homes in 1880, rural areas possessed no electric light well into the twentieth century. Completing the job became a goal of the United States government under President Franklin Roosevelt—one of the many public improvement projects initiated in his administration to revive an economy battered by the Depression and create jobs. The scheme involved building massive dams and developing other hydro-electric power projects, especially the Tennessee Valley Authority (TVA). With available power, the government could complete the electrification of America and provide basic amenities—heat, water and light—to outlying areas.

REA sketches

These are preliminary sketches Beall drew for the REA Series One posters, 1937.

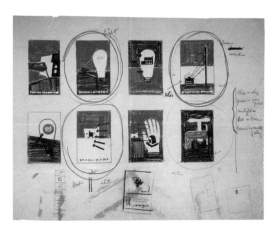

In 1937, Bill Phillips, an information officer for the REA, hired Beall, whom he had met through George Bijur, to communicate the benefits of electricity to citizens in regions such as Appalachia. The classic series of large format (30 x 40 inches) posters that resulted received national and international recognition. Beall designed three sets of six silk-screened posters for the REA over a period of four years. Series One includes *Farm Work*, *Heat … Cold*, *Radio*, *Running Water* and *Wash Day*. Their graphic simplicity and flat, unfussy, illustrative elements were appropriate for an audience with minimal reading skills and recalled the public posters designed by the Russian Constructivists twenty years earlier. For the second series, produced in 1939, and which included *Boy and Girl on Fence*, *Here It Comes*, *It's Fine For Us* and *When I Think Back*, Beall's visual language, marked by his experiments with photomontage, had become more complex. The third set, designed in 1941, the year the U.S. entered World War II, makes references to national defense, with titles such as *A Better Home*, *A Turn of the Hand*, *Power on the Farm* and *Rural Industries*. This group is the most visually intricate, with angled typography, patterns of color bars, dots, and silhouetted photographs.

REA Series Two poster, 1939
Two Kids on a Fence
Lester Beall did all the original photography for these posters. The hand-retouched silhouetted prints are in the RIT collection.

REA Series Three poster, 1941
Power for Defense
The final poster set showed that America was preparing for war and that electrification was essential for the war effort.

Experimental photography, c. 1938
Lester Beall used photography as a major imaging resource in his graphic design. He was regularly making experimental photographic images both in the studio and in the darkroom. He would frequently apply these images in his commercial design projects.

The posters have since become icons in the history of graphic design. As design writer Jerome Snyder remarked in 1972: "Beall demonstrated with these posters that the language of communication was not necessarily bound to timeworn clichés and literal conventions. An expanding world of science, technology and manufacturing had generated rising expectations that called for a new graphic industry, succinct of statement and visually attuned to the increasing velocity of American life."

Holding Vasari's belief that design is the "annunciating principle in all creative processes," Beall felt that the artist should be interested in many creative forms and open to motivation from many sources. Most often his chosen form of expression was drawing, painting or photography. He loved the female figure as a subject, although he occasionally worked with other forms, both representational and abstract. His visual vocabulary continued to be enriched by the painters whose works he had studied at the Chicago Art Institute and on his own: Klee, Picasso, Braque, Matisse, Miró, Derain and, especially at this time, Arp. He was particularly affected by the graphic quality of Matisse's canvasses, saying: "Picasso is a great artist but Matisse is a great painter."

Experimental photography, c. 1938
European avant-garde photographers such as Man Ray and Moholy-Nagy were influences on Beall's approach to photography. Throughout his career Beall would find creative inspiration from the female model in his photography, painting and drawing.

Beall's own painting and drawing was a way for him to get closer to his inner feelings. He treated his personal art very seriously and with intensity: not simply as a hobby or an emotional release, but as a need. He felt that when the designer takes "his color and his form and texture and he feels, in a sense, beneath the surface of these elements, then he has really accomplished something and is on his way to developing a style of his own." This form of invention fed his creative spirit and kept him in touch with the earliest roots of his career. Throughout his life, the vitality of feelings that emerged from his art was critical in stimulating his most effective personal graphic design work, and this was especially the case during the 1930s when his design office was small and there was a more distinctive, personal quality to the work it produced. In 1939, Beall wrote that, "modern typography and graphic design cannot occupy itself better than through an intensive study of modern abstract painting." The fact that much of his work was done in the service of advertising enhanced this process. Beall became troubled later in life with the pervasive notion that the graphic designer is in a world apart from the fine artist. Like Herbert Bayer, the Bauhaus artist who was an important influence on him, Beall was adamant about making no distinction between fine and applied arts in his career.

In 1938, Beall took on a project that was pivotal in changing his approach from conventional commercial illustration to modern design, particularly through his use of photomontage. Working with the writer L. Sandusky on an article for *PM* magazine called "The Bauhaus Tradition and the New Typography," Beall was able to select and format illustrations from Sandusky's personal collection. This was a chance to work with a scholar of the avant-garde and get close to original artworks that he probably had never seen before. Among the artists, designers and architects featured in Sandusky's article were Kandinsky, Archipenko, Gropius, El Lissitzky, Moholy-Nagy, Teige, Tschichold, Renner and Bayer. Beall saw their work as "only guideposts indicating characteristics which later fused themselves into the artists' creations." He saw this progressive work not as "standing out in blatant discord" to the prevailing styles of the time "but rather having a subtle effect as an emotionally digested influence."

Sterling *Photo Engraving* brochure 1938

This spread shows the application of Beall's experimental photography work. Note his technique of using a symmetrical format that was carefully contrasted with asymmetric elements.

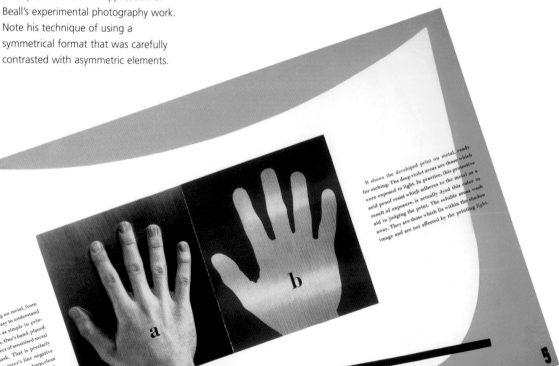

B shows the developed print on metal, ready for etching. The deep violet areas are those which were exposed to light. In practice, this protective acid proof resist which adheres to the metal as a result of exposure, is actually dyed this color to aid in judging the print. The soluble areas wash away. They are those which lie within the shadow image and are not affected by the printing light.

a

b

aphic printing on metal, from
, is not too easy to understand
, although it is as simple in prin-
, pictured at A. One's hand, placed,
tact with a sheet of sensitized metal
act as a mask. That is precisely
engraver's line negative
ork.

5

Self-Promotion advertisement, 1945

Beall was one of the important American synthesizers of Modernism. This ad represented the influence of Surrealism in his work as he replaces his head with the bold letter B.

Three years later, Beall wrote an article for *American Printer* magazine called "Design as Applied to Advertising." Here he articulated the influence of European modern art on his design process and launched into a theory of design based on planar forms first made popular by the Russian El Lissitzky in the early 1920s and then by Paul Klee in the 1930s. Pointing out that the "graphic arts and typography, like modern painting, are concerned with surface or plane design or organization," Beall wrote: "contemporary graphic design is dependent upon a visual consideration of three dimensionality, even though it is actually two dimensional. Planes (the illusion of three dimensionality) in graphics are established by form, color and texture. The receding and/or projecting properties of each design element can be altered by changing its form, texture and color. To insure the workability of a design, one must take care that no one of the established planes becomes completely disassociated from the others. The reason for this is that properly related planes make a design 'work,' while improperly related planes create confusion and a sense of 'busyness' that contributes markedly to the inefficiency of the design and therefore of the projected method."

***Hacia La Victoria* (Road to Victory), 1942–1943**

This two-page spread is from a publication Beall designed for Nelson Rockefeller. Printed in Spanish, it was intended to unify the nations of Central and South America with the Allies during World War II.

Freedom Pavilion poster, 1939

This was a prototype for a poster promoting the German Pavilion at the New York World's Fair. The redundancy between the figure and the Statue of Liberty created a powerful message.

***Fortune* magazine covers, 1947, 1946**
These covers exemplified Beall's method of
using a layering technique in compositions.

This analytical approach, which Beall found useful as a unifying method for much of his montage work from the period, was not to be understood as an expression of rules or axioms, he said, but as a tool. Seventeen years later, when he designed a corporate identity "style book" for Connecticut General Life Insurance Company in 1958, he offered another description of this approach in a simpler version, illustrated by a diagram. A style manual for a corporate identity might seem like an odd place to present design theory, but the presentation was consistent with Beall's career-long efforts to represent creative approaches analytically. Looked at in the light of both the *American Printer* article and the Connecticut General style manual, Beall's work of the 1930s and 1940s, including his 1947 cover for *Fortune* magazine, shows a direct application of the theory.

The 1939 World's Fair in New York was a hothouse of progressive design and architecture. Many important designers, who were also Beall's competitors—Donald Deskey, Paul Rand, Joseph Binder, Ladislav Sutnar and Will Burtin—contributed posters, guidebooks and exhibition designs. Beall was commissioned to create a poster for The Freedom Pavilion, a structure that was to house presentations about Germany, until Hitler's aggression in Europe on the eve of World War II led to the project's demise. Though the pavilion was never built, the poster, in prototype form, is an outstanding example of graphic design from the event. Beall's use of thrust and counter-thrust—angled photographs and white reversed line—creates tension. The Statue of Liberty symbolically balances the silhouetted photograph of the crying girl and the strong background colors supplement the imagery.

What's New cover, 1939

This complex image was created as a cover for *What's New*, a publication of Abbott Laboratories. Note that Beall has inverted the normal size relationships, placing the largest form of the woman's face behind the figure of the skater. This kind of visual ambiguity created interest and impact in his work.

In 1939, Beall also began the work that confirmed his reputation as one of the century's most innovative designers and launched a tradition continued by Will Burtin and George Giusti: the design of pharmaceutical promotions for Abbott Laboratories. His first project involved a cover design for the drug company's magazine, *What's New?*, on the topic of fever. Beall decided to photograph a nude model next to a beautiful white-washed branch. The branch, part of an old set-up for a still life, was on loan from the photographer/designer Herbert Matter. To suggest the idea of fever, Beall posed the model's hand on her head and partially solarized the branch. (His use of solarization, which involves manipulation of the film in controlled light during development, was experimental for him, and he and his staff were excited by the results.) *What's New?* was possibly the first house organ produced for a pharmaceutical company, and Beall believed it to be an important development in what was the golden age of pharmaceutical advertising, when companies had generous budgets to produce lavish promotional tools.

Later that year, *Gebrauchsgraphik*, the German magazine of advertising and graphic design, described Beall as, "the typical representative of those definitely intellectual artists whose creative work is based less upon spontaneity than upon reflection. His work displays an almost mathematical accuracy and architectonic clarity; one feels in looking at it that it has been executed with careful consideration and with a feeling of responsibility. Further it reveals a perfect command of the typographical medium and an unerring feeling for the proper arrangement of surfaces."

One of the signature projects of his professional life was a publication for another pharmaceutical company. In 1944, he began designing *Scope* magazine for the Upjohn pharmaceutical company in Kalamazoo, Michigan. Published bi-monthly, *Scope* was distributed to the medical profession and other health workers. The magazine covered a variety of subjects, from specific maladies and the drugs with which they were treated to acupuncture and art. Each issue began and ended with advertisements for Upjohn products, such as Unicap vitamins, which Beall also designed. His addition of color and arrows to the typography and geometric shapes created tasteful marketing messages that were compatible with the editorial pages.

Scope* magazine cover, 1947

This front and back cover for Upjohn Pharmaceutical's magazine *Scope* showed Beall's application of experimental photography. The image of the face is ambiguous with positive on one side and negative on the opposite side.

Beall's creative freedom was unparalleled in his (and almost any other designer's) career and was a tribute to the trust he inspired in his clients. According to his wife, Dorothy, he designed issues and sent them off to the printer without even showing them to Upjohn's management. *Scope* also afforded Beall opportunities to do experimental work with photography. He continued to show that the versatility of the medium gave the graphic designer a moving and powerful instrument.

Yet despite the freedom it allowed, the job was difficult and demanding. *Scope*'s Dr. A. Garrard Macleod, was slow to organize each issue and get copy to the designer, but demanded it remain on schedule, and it took some time before Beall established any credibility with his editor. He nevertheless looked back on the seven years of designing the magazine as "very exciting from so many different angles: the design and layout, the typography and the opportunity of interpreting in terms of photographs, drawings or paintings. It was the epitome of a designer's desire for freedom of expression."

In 1940, Beall had a goal to "pave the way for a new visual approach … a living dynamic approach that leaves no question as to its position or strength." That he realized this goal by extending the influence of the Bauhaus and New Typography movement to America is affirmed by L. Sandusky, who writes that Beall "maintained the integrity of these movements for clients of American printing, commercial photography and advertising design." A Museum of Modem Art publication stated, "The early work of such talented designers as Lester Beall is filled with this mixture of new ideas but soon the ideas were assimilated. An entirely new spirit was infused into American graphic design."

Scope magazine cover, 1948
Beall's cover for *Scope* represented his continued interest in a layering technique of image formulation. This *Scope* cover was one of his most well-known and highly praised cover designs.

Photograph, c. 1938
This image shows the influence
of the European avant-garde on
Beall's experimental studio photographs
in the 1940s.

Advertisement for George Bijur, Inc.
Beall's agent, George Bijur, hired him
to design trade advertisements.
Beall saw these jobs as great opportunities
for using his experimental photographs.

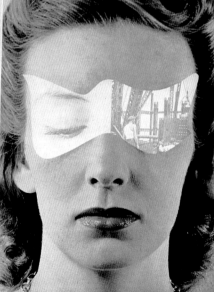

Pássaros da morte. Deslizam suave mas, terrivelmente, semeando a carnificina e o horror das chamas. "Aí, vão as balas para as tuas entranhas".

Hacia La Victoria (Road to Victory) 1942–1943

This publication, done in 1942, showed Beall's effective use of dramatic contrast in the treatment of the photographic imagery.

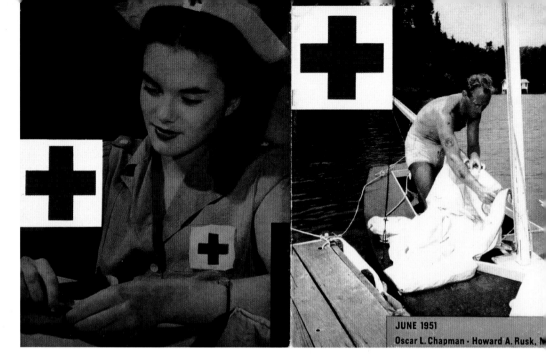

JUNE 1951
Oscar L. Chapman · Howard A. Rusk, N

Red Cross Magazine cover, 1951
Beall's cover designs for this magazine integrated strongly recognized symbols and appropriate photography.

Modern Pioneers in Peoria, 1937
This two-page spread showed Beall's masterful unification of type and image.

Scope magazine advertisement, 1947
In the late 1940s Beall's designs for Upjohn's *Scope* magazine frequently featured imaginative manipulation of photographs, color and typography.

cebēfortis

Only part of a surgical repair is done by the surgeon. When the surgeon has finished his repair of the gross structure, the cells of the body still have the infinitely more intricate task of repairing the minute structures. Like the surgeon they must have the equipment needed for the job. Vitamin C and the B vitamins are needed in abundance for this metabolic rehabilitation.

each tablet of Cebēfortis®contains:

Thiamine Hydrochloride
(B₁)   5.0 mg.

Riboflavin (B₂)   5.0 mg.

Pyridoxine Hydrochloride
(B₆)   5 mg.

Calcium Pantothenate
              5.0 mg.

Nicotinic Acid Amide
(Nicotinamide)   50.0 mg.

Ascorbic Acid (C) 150.0 mg.

Supplied in bottles of
100 and 500.

BEALL'S TIMELINE

1903–1969	LESTER THOMAS BEALL
1903	Born, Kansas City, Missouri, March 14, 1903 Family moved to St. Louis, Missouri
1903–1925	Spent summers in Ewing, Missouri with maternal grandparents
1910	Lived in St. Joseph, Missouri; Family moved to Chicago
1912–1926	Lived at 426 East 50TH Street, Chicago
1921	Received amateur radio station license
1922	Graduated Lane Technical School; attends University of Chicago
1922–1926	Appeared in semi-professional theater while a student at University of Chicago; Contemplated acting career with friend Will Geer; Decided upon career in visual arts
1926	Graduated from the University of Chicago
1927–1930	Started career in Chicago as a freelancer; Opened Chicago office
1928	Married Dorothy Miller
1929	Son Lester Beall, Jr. born on October 26, 1929
1930	Did first photography
1929–1931	Studied at Ryerson Memorial Library, Art Institute of Chicago; Became aware of the European avant-garde art and design; Sought "new direction" for his career

EARLY 1930S	Had design office on 31ST floor of 333 Building, Michigan Avenue
1932	Met Fred Hauck, BBDO Interests shifted from illustration to typography
1933	Designed first mural at the Chicago Century of Progress Joined Art Directors Club of Chicago
1934	Had design office with Fred Hauck Purchased first Leica camera; Did photograms Won award for illustration at the Chicago Art Directors Club Exhibited at New York Art Directors Club Gave talk at STA, *New Foundations for Layout* On trip East, visited Charles Coiner at N.W. Ayer, Philadelphia
MID-1930S	Involved as founding member of Chicago 27 Gave talk to STA, *Bauhaus and Moholy-Nagy*
1935	Won award at the STA annual exhibit Awarded three blue ribbons by New York Art Director's Club Daughter Joanna born, August 17, 1935 Moved to New York City ahead of family to begin practice Met Gil Tompkins; met George Bijur, CBS; designed first package
1936	Family reunited and lived in Wilton, Connecticut Two Gold Medal awards from New York Art Directors Club
1937	Exhibited REA posters at Museum of Modern Art Cover and feature article in *PM magazine*; Hired first employees
1938	Co-authored article with L. Sandusky, "The Bauhaus and the New Typography;" Article on Beall in *Gebrauschgraphik* Work shown in *Arts et Métiers Graphiques*, Vols. 61, 63, 65 Did photograms and experimental photography Designed series No. 2 of REA posters

1938–1939	Moved office to 580 Fifth Avenue; Firm called *Lester Beall*
1939	Work shown in *Arts et Métiers Graphiques*, Vol. 68
1941	Designed series No. 3 of REA posters
1942	Exhibited in *Advance Guard of Advertising Artists* show at A-D Gallery, New York (with Bayer, Carlu, Kepes, Kauffer, Matter, Moholy-Nagy, Rand and Sutnar); *Norte* article on Beall
1944	Designed first *Scope* for Upjohn
1945	One man show at A-D Gallery, New York Gold medal for fine arts at New York Art Directors Club
1948	Moved office to 60 Sutton Place South Exhibited in one-man show at Society of Illustrators, New York Art Directors Club of Chicago award for Marshall Field ads Beall's mother, Effie Kendall Thomas Beall, dies
1949, 1950	Bought Dumbarton Farm; moved to Dumbarton Farm
1951	First trip to Europe Gave talk at International Advertising Conference, London
1952	Opened office at Dumbarton Farm
1954	Visiting Graphic Artist at Yale University
1955	Closed office in New York Alliance Graphique Internationale exhibit, Paris Visiting Graphic Artist at Yale University
1956	Produced *Dumbarton Farm–A Place in the Country* booklet Produced *Music Sphere* for ALCOA Firm called "Lester Beall Design Group" Visiting Graphic Artist at Yale University

1958	Began work for International Paper Company
1959	Talk at Typography USA Conference, New York
1960	Incorporated business (June); firm called *Lester Beall Inc.*
1962	Produced *Lester Beall*, promotional booklet One-man exhibit, *The Graphic Work of Lester Beall* at American Institute of Graphic Arts, New York
1963	Beall's father, Walter Miles Beall, died
1965	Lester Beall became ill
1969	Lester Beall died (June 20, 1969)
1972	Studio and barns at Dumbarton Farm sold Inducted into Hall of Fame, New York Art Director's Club
1974	Lester Beall's personal fine arts and design library sold to Museum of Fine Arts, Houston, Texas
1983	House at Dumbarton Farm, personal literature collection sold
1986	Dorothy Miller Beall died Lester Beall Archive donated to Rochester Institute of Technology
1993	Lester Beall honored with AIGA Lifetime Achievement Award
1996	Book *Lester Beall–Trailblazer of American Graphic Design* written by R. Roger Remington and published by W.W. Norton and Company
1996	Exhibit of Lester Beall work at Reinhold-Brown Gallery
1997	Article on Lester Beall by R. Roger Remington in *Eye* Magazine

COLOPHON

Design   Bruce Ian Meader

Production   Amelia Hugill-Fontanel and Marnie Soom, assistant

Typefaces   Sabon designed by Jan Tschichold
and Frutiger designed by Adrian Frutiger

Paper   TriPine Dull text, Simwhite cover

Printing   Phoenix Asia